On The Road to Heaven

Rev. Wiley E. Shelley

Book Number I
I Stake My Claim

Book Number II
On The Road to Heaven

Reverend Wiley E. Shelby

Electric Tactics

Monroe, Michigan

On the Road to Heaven

Copyright © 2023 by Wiley Shelby

ISBN: 978-0-9830859-4-2

Library of Congress Control Number: 2023936941

All Bible quotations are from the King James Version.

Cover illustration by Cassie Stetson.

Photos courtesy Sandra Turner. Used with permission.

Illustrations courtesy Stock Photo Secrets. Used under license.

Contents

ACKNOWLEDGEMENTS

Thanks to many who helped make this book a reality.

My daughter, Debbie Godfrey, typed the text into the computer from my handwritten manuscript. Her daughter Jessica also helped with typing and printing off drafts.

My step-daughter, Sandra Turner, took many of the photographs and offered much helpful advice. Her husband Tom provided practical assistance and moral support.

My step-son, Mark Johansen, formatted the book for printing and assisted with the mechanics of publication.

My step-daughter, Cassie Stetson, scanned in photos and drew the cover illustration, as well as supplying the poem "Cabin Creek".

My wife, Ruth Shelby, spent many hours proof-reading and making corrections.

Thanks to my family for their contributions of poems, songs, testimonials, and more. Special thanks to Dwayne Shelby for the song, **I'll Take the Road to Heaven**. He wrote this as a young teenager and it was the idea for this book and title.

Isaiah 61:1-3

The Spirit of the LORD God is upon me; because the LORD hath anointed me to preach good tidings unto the meek; He hath sent me to bind up the brokenhearted, to proclaim liberty to the captives, and the opening of the prison to them that are bound;

To proclaim the acceptable year of the Lord, and the day of vengeance of our God; To comfort all that mourn;

To appoint unto them that mourn in Zion, to give unto them beauty for ashes, the oil of joy for mourning, the garment of praise for the spirit of heaviness; that they might be called trees of righteousness, the planting of the LORD, that He might be glorified.

Introduction: In the Beginning

I want to start from the beginning: God loved His creation from the start! That is why He created it—to share with His creation. He loved Adam and Eve so much that he would walk in the garden in the cool of the day, just to have fellowship with them. When Adam and Eve disobeyed God's instructions by eating the forbidden fruit, they brought sin on all mankind. They selfishly ate fruit from the tree of knowledge of good and evil instead of choosing the tree of Life. There were other trees in the garden, but we have a rebellious nature, and God gives us choice.

God loved the whole world so much that He gave His only son to die on the old wooden cross to pay our sin debt. We are born sinners, but God had a plan of redemption from the beginning. God loved us first, even before we loved Him. God is not dead. He still wants to commune with us.

Jesus was part of that plan. He gave His all because of that sinful fall in the garden. He took on our sin debt that we could never pay. He came down from Heaven, suffered and died so we can have an eternal home in Heaven after we die. Jesus is not on the cross anymore. It is finished! They took Him down and put Him in a tomb, but on the third day, He arose from the grave. The women went to the tomb and found it empty. The angel told them Jesus was not there, He arose and He lives forevermore. Hallelujah!

Jesus, who had no sin, lived and died and rose again to pay our sin debt. The debt we could not pay. Only the blood of Jesus, dying on the cross would do. We must tell the world, "Jesus is the way-maker so that lost souls might have Eternal life." It is our job as Christians to tell them who He is. From the beginning, Jesus is and was and is to come -- The Way, The Truth and The Life. No man can come to the Father, but by Him. He is The Only Way to Heaven. He is your salvation and the only way to escape the flames of Hell. Believe and ask Him to come into your heart and take away your sin. He will not turn you away.

From the beginning was the Holy Trinity: The Father God, The Son of God, and the Holy Spirit.

Jesus was born of a virgin. The Holy Spirit hovered over Mary just as He hovered over the waters in the beginning. She became pregnant with God's Only Son. He came down to earth and walked among men for 33 ½ years. He died on the cross, shedding His blood to pay our sin debt that we could not pay. Without the shedding of His blood, there would not be a second birth. Jesus told Nicodemus, "You must be born again, a spiritual birth." We don't understand it all, but it is God's Word. God cannot lie. His Word is True.

Now is the appointed time. We are all born in sin and have decisions to make about the welfare of our souls. We must be made Holy through our Lord Jesus Christ in order to have eternal life. We must have salvation, not just religion. There are different religions but only one salvation. Jesus shed His blood on the cross to wash away our sins. If we want to share the glory of God, the only way is Jesus: ask, seek, knock. Believe, repent, and ask Him to save you from your sins.

Choose you this day whom you will serve: Eternal life in the heavenly realm or Everlasting death in a burning fire.

> Matthew 7:7-8 (and it is also recorded in Luke 11:9-10)
>
> Ask and it shall be given you; seek and ye shall find; knock, and it shall be opened unto you: For every one that asketh receiveth; and he that seeketh findeth; and to him that knocketh it shall be opened.
>
> Luke 13:24
>
> Straight is the gate. Strive to enter in at the gate. For many, I say unto you, will seek to enter in, and shall not be able.
>
> Matthew 7:13-14
>
> Enter ye in at the strait gate: for wide is the gate, and broad is the way, that leadeth to destruction, and many there be which go in thereat:

John 11:25-26

Jesus said unto her, "I am the resurrection, and the life: he that believeth in me, though he were dead, yet shall he live: And whosoever liveth and believeth in me shall never die. Believeth thou this?"

Numbers 20:17

Let us pass, I pray thee, through thy country: we will not pass through the fields, or through the vineyards, neither will we drink of water of the wells: we will go by the King's high way, we will not turn to the right hand nor to the left, until we have passed thy borders.

As the poem below says, it really matters to me what God says at the end of my journey; and I have heard "those who walk with God are bound to be out of step with the world." So, my prayer is, after reading this book, you will choose to walk with God.

It matters not what others say

In ridicule or fun,

I want to live that I may hear,

Him say to me, "Well done."

Chapter 1: Starting your Journey

Walking with God

With the issues we currently face, including confusion in the churches and in its religious leaders, doubt and insecurity that plagues us -- we could become paralyzed with fear. We could join the ungodly and forget it all. Or we can seek assurance in the midst of uncertainty as we walk with God in peace.

How? By faith in God, who made a deliverance plan for man before the world began. We apply His Truth in our lives.

Psalm 23

The Lord is my shepherd; I shall not want.

He maketh me to lie down in green pastures: he leadeth me beside the still waters.

He restoreth my soul: he leadeth me in the paths of righteousness for his name's sake.

Yea, though I walk through the valley of the shadow of death, I will fear no evil: for thou art with me; thy rod and thy staff they comfort me.

Thou preparest a table before me in the presence of mine enemies: thou anointest my head with oil; my cup runneth over.

> Surely goodness and mercy shall follow me all
> the days of my life: and I will dwell in the house
> of the Lord for ever.

Let's break this down into three important assurances:

1.   The Lord is my Shepherd: He is our personal Shepherd. We belong to Him! He bought us with His blood. No one can pluck us out of His hands. Only those who are saved can claim Him as their Shepherd.

John 14:27 says, "Peace I leave with you, my peace I give unto you: not as the world giveth, give I unto you. Let not your heart be troubled, neither let it be afraid."

2.   I shall not want: He is our providing Shepherd. One of the primary tasks of the Shepherd is to feed and water the flock. Green pastures and still waters! Does He not promise to supply our needs according to His riches in Glory? He will give you the desires of your heart and He restores your soul!

He is our pardoning Shepherd, retrieving us from our foolish wanderings. He guides us in the right paths. He not only forgives our sin when we ask but restores our fellowship with Him.

3.   I will fear no evil: He is our protecting Shepherd. Like shepherds of old, He leads us from mountain to mountain, through valleys, often dark and dangerous! Even through the valley of the shadow of death but we never walk alone.

In the midst of all this turmoil, unrest, and violence ... We are assured that His goodness and mercy will follow us to the grave.

God Is Able to Deliver

Holy Scripture give us many examples of God's
       deliverance:

God delivered Israel through the Red Sea.
God delivered Daniel from the Lion's Den.
God delivered Shadrach, Meshach, and Abednego from
       the fiery furnace.
God delivered Jonah from the belly of the whale.
God delivered Peter from prison.
God delivered Paul from storms and shipwreck.
God delivered Paul and Silas from jail.
God delivered Lazarus and Jairus's daughter from
       death itself.

God is able to deliver us from sin. He delivered me
from my sins. He can deliver you from your sins if you
only ask Him. Recall the words of the old hymn …
"Trust and obey, for there is no other way … To be
happy in Jesus, but to trust and obey."

    Psalm 18:2

    The LORD is my rock, and my fortress, and my
    deliverer; my God, my strength, in whom I will
    trust; my buckler, and the horn of my salvation,
    and my high tower.

Three Men Dying on A Cross

In Luke 23:34-44, we learn there were three men dying on the cross that day:

- One died for our sins

- One died in his own sins

- One died forgiven for his sins

Jesus Christ died for our sins.

The crowd was insulting. He had been beaten and abused horribly, yet He prayed to the Father for them, saying, "Father forgive them for they know not what they do."

The soldiers were not concerned about His suffering. They divided up his clothes and cast lots for them. People stood staring at Him. Some crying, some laughing, some making fun of Him, saying, "He saved others, let Him save Himself, if He be the Christ, the Chosen One of God." Soldiers mocked Him, offering Him vinegar to drink. (v 40) One of the thieves confessed his own sin and criticized his companion (v 41). He proclaimed that Christ was sinless. (v 42). He showed wonderful faith in Jesus and called Him "Lord." He made a model prayer. He accepted Christ as his personal savior and was saved right on the cross. (v 43).

Jesus said to him, "Verily, I say to you, today shalt thou be with Me in paradise." The moment he died he was in paradise with his Savior.

II Corinthians 5:8

We are confident, I say, and willing rather to be absent from the body, and to be present with the LORD.

He will forgive your sins and save you the moment you pray to him, repenting for your sins and asking Him to come into your heart. You must believe that He died on the cross for you and believe that He rose again three days later and is now seated at the right hand of the Father. He said, "Ye must be born again to enter into the Kingdom of God." That is a spiritual birth. When you trust Christ to be your Savior and Lord, the Holy Spirit comes into you and helps you live for Him.

Who is Jesus?

Matthew 22:41-46

While the Pharisees were gathered together, Jesus asked them, saying, What think ye of Christ? Whose son is he?

They say unto him, The son of David.

He saith unto them, How then doth David in spirit call him Lord, saying, The LORD said unto my Lord, Sit thou on my right hand, till I make thine enemies thy footstool? If David then call him Lord, how is he his son?

And no man was able to answer him a word, neither durst any man from that day forth ask him any more questions.

All in All

Who is Jesus? Outside of Christ, nothing matters. The entire Bible is His person and His plan. The purpose of life is to know Him and enjoy Him forever. We look forward to the Great Homecoming when King Jesus will reign and live among His people. He is my All in All.

Where Jesus is, there is no disappointment

John 14:1-6

Let not your heart be troubled: ye believe in God, believe also in me.

In my Father's house are many mansions: if it were not so, I would have told you. I go to prepare a place for you. And if I go and prepare a place for you, I will come again, and receive you unto myself; that where I am, there ye may be also. And whither I go you know, and the way ye know.

Thomas saith unto him, Lord, we know not whither thou goest; and how can we know the way?

Jesus saith unto him, I am the way, the truth, and the life: no man cometh unto the Father, but by me.

He is The Balm of Gilead

Jeremiah 8:22

Is there no balm in Gilead: is there no physician there? Why then is not the health of the daughter of my people recovered?

He is The Bright and morning Star

Rev 22:16

I Jesus have sent mine angel to testify unto you these things in the churches. I am the root and the offspring of David, and the bright and morning star.

He is The Builder of the Church

Matthew 16:18

And I say also unto thee, that thou art Peter, and upon this rock I will build my church; and the gates of hell shall not prevail against it.

He is The Bread of God

John 6:33

For the bread of God is he which cometh down from heaven, and giveth life unto the world.

He is The Brightness of His Glory

Hebrews 1:3

Who being the brightness of his glory, and the express image of his person, and upholding all things by the word of his power, when he had by himself purged our sins, sat down on the right hand of the Majesty on High.

He is The Blood Covenant

Luke 22:20

Likewise also the cup after supper, saying This cup is the new testament in my blood, which is shed for you.

He is The Bridegroom

Rev 19:7

Let us be glad and rejoice, and give honor to him: for the marriage of the Lamb is come and his wife hath made herself ready.

What Does the Bible Say About Being Saved?

Many times, we hear what people say about "the Way" of salvation, but rarely hear what God's Word says. Here, as plain as the nose on your face, is the plan of salvation explained in Romans, from Gods Word:

1. We are all Sinners.

Romans 3:10

There is none righteous, no, not one.

Romans 3:23

For all have sinned, and come short of the glory of God.

2. The price of sin is death.

Romans 5:12

Wherefore, as by one man sin entered into the world, and death by sin; and so death passed upon all men, for that all have sinned.

Romans 6:23

For the wages of sin is death; but the gift of God is eternal life through Jesus Christ our Lord.

3. Jesus Christ paid that price.

Roman 5:8

But God commendeth his love toward us, in that, while we were yet sinners, Christ died for us.

4. What must we do to be saved?

Romans 10:9

That if thou shalt confess with thy mouth the Lord Jesus, and shalt believe in thine heart that God hath raised him from the dead, thou shalt be saved.

Romans 10:10

For with the heart man believeth unto righteousness, and with the mouth confession is made unto salvation.

Romans 10:13

For whosoever shall call upon the name of the Lord shall be saved.

Remember: Confess, Believe, and Ask -- and thou shalt be saved!

Proverbs 3:5-7

Trust in the Lord with all thine heart,

And lean not unto thine own understanding. In all thy ways acknowledge Him,

And He shall direct thy paths.

Be not wise in thine own eyes:

Fear the LORD, and depart from evil.

Spiritual Birth

God wants you to believe His Word and receive Jesus Christ as your personal Savior. If you do that, He will do these wonderful things for you.

God has received you as His child!

John 1:12

Yet to all who did receive him, to those who believed in his name, he gave the right to become children of God.

God has forgiven your sins!

Acts 10:43

To him give all the prophets witness, that through his name whosoever believeth in him shall receive remission of sins.

God has given you the free gift of eternal life!

Romans 6:23

For the wages of sin is death, but the gift of God is eternal life in Christ Jesus our Lord.

God has saved you from an eternity in hell!

Romans 10:13

For everyone who calls on the name of the Lord will be saved.

Why Would You?

Matthew 10:37

He that loveth father or mother more than me
is not worthy of me: and he that loveth son or
daughter more than me is not worthy of me.

Why would you love the things of this world more
than God, seeing how much God has done for
you?
Why would you love father, mother, son or daughter
more than Christ?
Why would you turn away from the cross after all he
gave for you?
Why would you turn away from the cross after seeing
the promises he has given you?
Why would you turn away from the cross after looking
at yourself?
Why would you not live for Him?
He loves you more than any person ever could!
He suffered and died to pay for your sins.
He promised to come again and take you to
Paradise, where there is no death or sickness.
You were a sinner, saved by Grace.

The High Cost of Low Standards

The high cost of low standards is bankrupting us. You can see this all around you. Sin is destroying people's lives. Drugs, drunkenness, cheap sex, greed, violence, the list goes on and on. The wages of sin is death, and we are receiving our wages paid in full. Even when Christians are not engaged in these sins themselves, we share in the responsibility. We failed to teach others to live right. It is our responsibility to teach by words and by example. We are supposed to be the light of the world.

> Matthew 5:14-15
>
> Ye are the light of the world. A city that is set on an hill cannot be hid.
>
> Neither do men light a candle, and put it under a bushel, but on a candlestick; and it giveth light unto all that are in the house.

Come Home, Prodigal

Read Luke 15:11-24.

A son was unhappy with his life with his father. He asked his dad for his part of the family inheritance immediately. The dad was not happy about it but gave it to him. The son quickly squandered the money. He wasted all that the father had given him on wild parties and reckless living.

When the money ran out, his friends abandoned him. Then, broke and alone, he thought about all he had while he was with his father. Even his father's servants lived better than he was living now! He would be better off going back home and living in the barn than his present life. Then he began to reason with himself and realized what was missing. Even if he had to live in the barn, he would be better than the way he was living now. So he swallowed his pride and went back home. He had a speech of apology all prepared.

What a wonderful Home Coming! His Father saw him away off. He ran to meet him and hugged him. He put a ring on his finger, a robe around his shoulders, and shoes on his feet. He had a fatted calf cooked for the celebration.

The Backslider returns to God the Father

John 14:1-3

Let not your heart be troubled: ye believe in God, believe also in me.

In my Father's house are many mansions: if it were not so, I would have told you. I go to prepare a place for you.

And if I go and prepare a place for you, I will come again, and receive you unto myself; that where I am, there ye may be also.

In the same way as Jesus told his disciples, God will love you, forgive you and welcome you to spend eternity with Him.

I am going to my heavenly home someday. It will be the final dwelling place for the saints of God. It is a place of beauty and joy. What a homecoming that will be, to see Christ, and family, and others we have loved! We will feast at God's table.

Three Kinds of People

The Bible tells of three kinds of people:

Natural Man, 1 Corinthians 2:14

He is spiritually blinded. He does not accept the things of the Spirit of God. These are foolishness to him. He is spiritually ignorant, cannot understand it because these things are spiritually appraised. He has a self-controlled life. His ego puts self on the throne and Christ outside his life. Results are discord and frustration.

Spiritual Man, 1 Corinthians 2:14-15

He is controlled and empowered by the Holy Spirit. He puts Christ on the Throne of his life and dethrones himself. He is in harmony, at peace, and loves God and man. He is spiritually minded. To be "spiritually" minded is life, whereas "Carnal" minded is death!

Carnal Man, 1 Corinthians 3:1-3

He is one who has received Christ -- but who lives defeated because he trusts in his own efforts. Remaining a baby in Christ, not growing, full of jealousy, strife, discord, frustration. Also living a self-controlled life.

Which one of the three do you want to be?

Avoiding Hell

The Bible says there is a real place of fire, literal burning hell, a place of torment and everlasting punishment. Jesus taught about hell:

> Matthew 5:22
>
> Ye have heard that it was said of the of old time, thou shalt not kill; and whosoever shall kill shall be in danger of the judgment; But I say unto you, That whosoever is angry with his brother without a cause shall be in danger of the judgment; and whosoever shall say to his brother, Raca, shall be in danger of the council: but whosoever shall say Thou fool, shall be in danger of hell fire.

Luke also quotes Jesus as saying:

> Luke 5:12
>
> But I will forewarn you whom ye shall fear: Fear him, which after he hath killed hath power to cast into hell; yea I say unto you Fear him.

He also told the parable of the rich man and the poor man, Lazarus, who died, as recorded in Luke 16:19-31. The poor man's soul was carried by the angels to spend eternity with Abraham. But the rich man's soul suffered torment and anguish in everlasting flames. He cried out to Abraham, pleading to send warnings back to his brothers so they can escape hell.

Abraham's reply is sobering and speaks volumes to unbelievers: "if they hear not Moses and the prophets, neither will they be persuaded, though one rose from the dead."

Hell is a **real** place, not merely the grave as some say. It is a place prepared for the devil and his angels.

Hell is a place where the wicked and all nations that forget God will be condemned to.

Hell is never full. It enlarges itself.

Hell is a place of memory.

Hell is a place of continued prayer meetings but too late.

Hell is mentioned more times in the Bible than Heaven.

Christ told Peter that the gates of hell shall not prevail against the church. The only way to escape hell is to be born again. The wise person will avoid hell; he will forsake sin and accept Christ as His Savior and go to live with Jesus.

Choose you this day whom you will serve.

God's Toolbox

1 Cor 1:27

> But God hath chosen the foolish things of the world to confound the wise; and God hath chosen the weak things of the world to confound the things which are mighty;

God chooses what tools to use to get our attention. He knows what he needs to teach us to depend on him.

We can see this in the story of Jonah. God told Jonah to preach to the people of Nineveh. Jonah didn't want to preach to Nineveh because he was afraid they would repent, and that God would then show them mercy. But he wanted Nineveh to suffer.

So, Jonah tried to run away from God. When God told him to go to Nineveh, instead he bought a ticket to Tarshish, in the opposite direction. God used a storm to get Jonah's attention. God used a fish to take him to Nineveh, where he had told him to go in the first place.

Jonah preached to Nineveh and then climbed up a hill looking over the city to watch what would happen. The people did repent and God had mercy and did not destroy them. Jonah was angry that God withheld his judgement.

Meanwhile Jonah was sitting under the hot sun on the hilltop. God used a gourd to shade him from the sun and give him relief. Then God used a worm to take the gourd away to teach him about disobedience.

The wind and sun got to Jonah. He had forgotten all about his own discipline and repentance. God reminded him of the mercy he had been shown and that God is in charge.

God had a full toolbox to use as the need arose.

God knows which tool to use on you and me when we backslide and need to turn around. Sometimes the tool is sharp and it hurts when God uses it on us. It might be a nasty neighbor, quarrelsome spouse, or rebellious child. It might be problems at the job or financial worries. Or it might be a fish!

God holds the tools. He knows which tools to use to shape and mold us into the image of Christ.

> Romans 12:1
>
> I beseech you brethren, by the mercies of God, that ye present your bodies a living sacrifice, holy, acceptable unto God, which is your reasonable service.
>
> Proverbs 29:18
>
> Where there is no vision, the people perish: but he that keepeth the law, happy is he.

Football with the Devil

Romans 12:21

Be not overcome of evil but overcome evil with good.

Imagine playing a football game against the Devil with your soul instead of a ball. You would never consider voluntarily giving the Devil possession, would you?

First, the way to make the team is to ask God to save you. God said, "Ask and it shall be given, Seek and you shall find, Knock and it shall be open to you. By faith, God will put you on His team. To stay active and improve your game, you must abide by His rules, and there are penalties too. His rules are the Ten Commandments. Jesus might have the handbook that explains basics such as "Love God, Love people". God wrote the rules. He owns the team. He is the coach and calls every move, not you. God is the captain, referee, timekeeper, and scorekeeper.

Remember the football here is your soul. Don't fumble the ball. You have it! Keep it clear. Let God call every move. Carry the ball, don't let the opponent have it! Run toward the Heavenly goal. Don't foul, faint, or fall by the wayside. Call a time out anytime to talk to God. He will be there for you. He said, 'I will never leave you or forsake you. I will go all the way with you even to the end of the world." Although you are going up against a powerful opponent (Satan), our God is the greatest power and has never lost a game. Even when Satan tackles, never give up! Keep your eyes fixed on the gates of Heaven. For the big homecoming game will be soon. Your trophies await. Christ is waiting to give you the crown of life in a beautiful Heaven where you will live with Him forever. Imagine a land with no sickness, no death, and sharing God's glory. You will not lose this game if you firmly place your (football) soul in God's hand.

Encouragement for a Troubled Heart

Encouragement comes only if you love the Word of God.

God is the God of all comfort.

When pressures get to you and all kinds of difficult time; dark times when pain and sorrow are unbearable, call on Him, Trust Him.

When the bottom drops out of your business, your job, or your world...

God is the God of all comfort.

Discouragement is one of the Devil's chosen tools against believers.

When you are discouraged, you will not grow. You will not be productive. You are a poor servant of God when you are discouraged. We cannot trust in ourselves, but must trust in the God of all comfort.

Encouragement is a comfort. The Holy Spirit is a comforter, a teacher, a leader, a guide. Attitudes change and your focus changes when the Holy Spirit lives in you.

> II Corinthians 1:3-7
>
> Blessed be God, even the Father of our Lord Jesus Christ, the Father of mercies, and the God of all comfort; Who comforteth us in all our tribulation, that we may be able to comfort

them which are in any trouble, by the comfort wherewith we ourselves are comforted of God.

For as the sufferings of Christ abound in us, so our consolation also aboundeth by Christ.

And whether we be afflicted, it is for your consolation and salvation, which is effectual in the enduring of the same sufferings which we also suffer: or whether we be comforted, it is for your consolation and salvation.

And our hope of you is steadfast, knowing, that as you are partakers of the sufferings, so shall you be also of the consolation.

Chapter 2: Start Building a Godly Home

Psalm 127:1

Unless the LORD builds the house, the builders labor in vain. Unless the LORD watches over the city, the guards stand watch in vain.

The Most Beautiful Thing in the World

There is an old story circulating about an artist's search for the most beautiful thing in the world. He wanted to capture this "thing" on canvas.

So, he first visited his pastor and asked, "What is the most beautiful thing in the world?"

"Faith," answered the pastor. "You can feel it in your church and especially find it at the altar." It must be more than a feeling, the artist thought.

Next, the artist asked a young bride the same question. "What is the most beautiful thing in the world?"

"Love," she replied. "Love builds poverty into riches, sweetens tears, and makes much of little. Without love there is no beauty."

Not satisfied, with her answer, the artist continued his search. A weary soldier answered his question, "Peace.

Peace is the most beautiful thing in the world. War is the ugliest; Wherever you find peace, you find beauty."

"Faith, love and peace. What does that look like? How can I paint them?" thought the artist as he approached his own front door. Entering the room, he recognized faith in the eyes of his children and love in the eyes of his wife. And there in his own home, he found the peace that love and faith had built. Now, he knew what the most beautiful thing in the world looked like. He indeed painted the picture of the most beautiful thing in the world. And when he had finished, he called it "HOME."

God's Discipline

Psalm 119:65-77

Thou hast dealt well with thy servant, O LORD, according unto thy word.

Teach me good judgment and knowledge: for I have believed thy commandments.

Before I was afflicted I went astray: but now have I kept thy word.

Thou art good, and doest good; teach me thy statutes.

The proud have forged a lie against me: but I will keep thy precepts with my whole heart.

Their heart is as fat as grease; but I delight in thy law.

It is good for me that I have been afflicted; that I might learn thy statutes.

The law of thy mouth is better unto me than thousands of gold and silver.

Thy hands have made me and fashioned me: give me understanding, that I may learn thy commandments.

They that fear thee will be glad when they see me; because I have hoped in thy word.

I know, O LORD, that thy judgments are right,
and that thou in faithfulness hast afflicted me.

Let, I pray thee, thy merciful kindness be for
my comfort, according to thy word unto thy
servant.

Let thy tender mercies come unto me, that I
may live: for thy law is my delight.

The Secret to Happiness

A woman called on her friend, "You always seem so
happy. Nothing ever seems to get you down. What
is your secret?"

Her friend replied, "Yes, there is a secret. I'm happy
to tell you about it. But you have to promise to share
the secret with others."

"The secret is ...that I have learned that there is
little I can do to make myself truly happy. I must
depend on God. I trust God to supply what I really
need. I don't need half of what I think I need. God
has never let me down. Since I learned that secret, I
have been happy."

The questioning woman thought, "that's too simple".
But after reflecting on her own life, she thought
about her attempts to find happiness. She thought a
bigger house would make her happy. So, she got a
bigger house, and it didn't. She thought a better job
would make her happy. But she got a better job, and
it didn't bring happiness. When did she realize her

greatest happiness? Sitting in the floor, time spent with her grandkids, playing games, eating pizza or reading a story, a simple gift from God.

Now you know the secret. We can't depend on people or things to make us happy. Only God in His infinite wisdom can do that. Trust Him to supply those simple gifts of life that bring happiness.

And now I pass the secret to you! So, once you get it, what will you do? Tell someone this secret, too! That God in His wisdom will take care of you! But it's not really a secret. We just have to believe it and do it...Really trust God in all things!

Fathers set the example for kids!

Leviticus 11:44-45

For I am the LORD your God: ye shall therefore sanctify yourselves, and ye shall be holy; for I am holy: neither shall ye defile yourselves with any manner of creeping thing that creepeth upon the earth.

For I am the LORD that bringeth you up out of the land of Egypt, to be your God: ye shall therefore be holy, for I am holy.

Leviticus 19:2

Speak unto all the congregation of the children of Israel, and say unto them, Ye shall be holy: for I the LORD your God am holy.

Well-chosen words are important, but a good example is better. See Genesis 22 for Abraham's fatherly example as he trusted God completely. Then examine the story in Luke 15 of the Prodigal's Homecoming, showing extravagant Fatherly love. Your children not only hear your words but they see you in action.

You may be well-known and admired for your talent or your job, but what kind of example are you setting for your children? They know if or when you read the Bible and pray. They see your priorities, if other things (like books, TV or internet) come first before God. They see how you treat their mom, the neighbors, and others. Fathers should set a godly tone at home and in public.

Point your children to Christ. He is the only foundation to meaningful living. Your children need to see your faith in action for all matters. When you start something finish it. The end is as important as the beginning to them. Paul said, "Run the race with patience." Finish the course.

Hebrews 12:1

Wherefore seeing we also are compassed about with so great a cloud of witnesses, let us lay aside every weight, and the sin which doth so easily beset us, and let us run with patience the race that is set before us, looking unto Jesus the author and finisher of our faith; who for the joy that was set before him endured the cross, despising the shame, and is set down at the right hand of the throne of God.

What Is a Father's Role?

A father is many things to his children and often is not appreciated. Most importantly, he is a godly example in the home:

- The Father is Provider: not always what you want but what you need.

- The Father is Protector: In times of storms, danger, fear, drugs/alcohol whatever may cause harm.

- The Father is a Priest: He has the privilege of coming to God on behalf of his family and to guide them in the way of Truth.

- The Father is Prophet: He foretells the Word of God to his children.

- The Father is Professor, Teacher, Doctor, Pastor: because he loves his children and guides them.

Trustworthy Precepts for a Father

1. He makes himself responsible for his child's behavior

2. He is never blinded by love from recognizing and correcting his child's weakness

3. He makes his child feel secure

4. He shares in his child's activities

5. He has his child's complete confidence

6. He is always available to help solve youthful problems

7. He doesn't demand absolute devotion ... he wins it from his child

8. He recognizes and accepts as largely his, the responsibility for his child's mental and spiritual development

9. He contributes to making the home the child's haven

10. He strives to be honest with his child

Encouraging Your Pastor

You may think of the pastor's job as being to encourage and support the members of his congregation. But, serving as a pastor, I know that your pastor needs encouragement and support too!

The importance of surrounding yourself with godly people, your community of faith (the church and extended family), cannot be overstated for their support, encouragement, prayers, etc.

Prayers, notes of thanks, or other encouraging words mean so much to pastors (and so do cute notes from kids that we receive!) Every church member should be praying for their pastor and all church leaders! Let others know you are praying for them!

As I write this book, this classic hymn comes to mind written over 100 years ago, ***Must Jesus Bear the Cross Alone***. Historically, Thomas Shepherd (1665-1739) is given credit for the original poem. Also found published in a collection of hymns by George M. Allen (1812-1877), the hymn with stanzas 2 and 3 added. Then Henry Ward Beecher (1813-1887), is credited with adding stanzas 4 and 5. Read these lyrics and think about the importance of carrying the cross.

Must Jesus Bear the Cross Alone

Must Jesus bear the cross alone,
And all the world go free?
No, there's a cross for everyone,
And there's a cross for me.

How happy are the saints above,
Who once went sorr'wing here!
But now they taste unmingled love,
And joy without a tear.

The consecrated cross I'll bear
Till death shall set me free;
And then go home my crown to wear,
For there's a crown for me.
Upon the crystal pavement down
At Jesus' pierced feet,
Joyful I'll cast my golden crown
And His dear Name repeat.

O precious cross! O glorious crown!
O resurrection day!
When Christ the Lord from heav'n comes down
And bears my soul away.

Source:library.timelesstruths.org/music/
Must_Jesus_Bear_the_Cross_Alone/umcdiscipleship.org.
History of Hymns: "Must Jesus Bear the Cross Alone", by
C. Michael Hawn.

Mark 8:34

Jesus said, "Whosoever will come after me, let him deny himself and take up his cross and follow Me.

Matthew 27:32

And as they *came out, they found a man of Cyrene, Simon by name: him they compelled to bear his cross.

to the Preacher
From: Stacy Colbent

Thank you for
Preaching at this
church.

A Prayer for My Pastor

Heavenly Father,

Let me be a pillar of strength to help hold up my pastor; and not a thorn in his flesh to sap his strength,

or a burden on his back to weigh him down.

Let me support him without striving to possess him.

Let me lift his hands without shackling them.

Let me give him any help so that he may devote more time to working for the salvation of others and less time to gratifying my vanity.

Let me work for him as he is the pastor of all the members; and not compel him to spend precious time in pleasing me.

Let me be unselfish in what I do for him and in what I ask him to do for me.

In Jesus Name I pray! AMEN.

The Pastor's Family

Your Pastor's wife and family are important to your church as well. They are an encouragement and helpers in the ministry to our LORD. Pray for them and show them your love too.

This recognition was given to both Mrs. Shelbys by West Side Baptist Church, Knoxville, TN.

My first wife, Imogene who passed away and is with the LORD; and also my present wife, Ruth, who is now serving by my side. I also thank them for being there when I and others needed them! They are vital workers in God's plan.

December 20, 2018

Dear Rev. Shelby

Last Thursday, Dec. 13th, I attended the gospel singing concert at North Knoxville Baptist Church. What a blessing we all received from "Eternal Vision." After the program I had the privilege of talking and listening to your son Mike tell about your family, and I was fortunate to purchase your book "I Stake My Claim."

West Side Baptist Church was my home church until I married in 1964. I remember you, Imogene, and your five children at the time. I also remember the Housewrights and Carl Knight.

After reading your wonderful book I learned what special children you raised.

It is so inspiring to read your book about the faith you and Imogene instilled in your children and grandchildren. I loved reading about their musical abilities and all the events in their lives. I wish I could have known them as they grew up, but life moved us in different directions.

God bless you for your ministries to so many people. Thank you for writing your book!

Sincerely,
Dalphine Owen Murphy
(My parents were Charles and Josie)

December 20, 2018

Dear Rev. Shelby,

Last Thursday, Dec. 13th, I attended the gospel singing concert at North Knoxville Baptist Church. What a blessing we all received from "Eternal Vision." After the program I had the privilege of talking and listening to your son Mike tell about your family, and I was fortunate to purchase your book, "*I Stake My Claim*."

West Side Baptist Church was my home church until I married in 1964. I remember you, Imogene, and your five children at the time. I also remember the Housewrights and Carl Knight.

After reading your wonderful book I learned what special children you raised. It is so inspiring to read your book about the faith you and Imogene instilled in your children and grandchildren. I loved reading about their musical abilities and all the events in their lives. I wish I could have known them as they grew up but life moved us in different directions.

God bless you for your ministries to so many people. Thank you for writing your book!

Sincerely,

Dalphene Owen Murphy

(My parents were Charles and Josie)

Dear Ruth and Wiley,

I could never thank you both enough for all you did for me while you were here. I really appreciate everything. Thanks for taking me all those places, and for all the work you did here at the house. I wish you all lived closer so we could see each other more often. I love you both very much, and I pray for you every day. I look forward to seeing you all in the Spring. Stay as long as you want to. I love having you.

Take care.
THANK YOU.
Love and God bless you,
Kathy Owen

I miss you so much. Thanks again.

I always welcome letters of encouragement like this! This sweet letter from a dear friend means so much to me. It not only encourages us but reminds me of the next story...

Light Not Needed

A blind lady named Kathy (not the same Kathy who wrote the letter above – two blind ladies both named Kathy is just a coincidence) worked with her hands making baskets and mats out of straw. She loved the Lord and attended every service at church with a friend who picked her up.

One Sunday, Kathy dropped $27 in the offering plate. Her friend was quite surprised and asked "Kathy, did you make a mistake? You put $27 in the offering. Surely you don't make enough money to be able to afford an offering of so much. And how did you come up with that odd amount?

"Oh, but I can," Kathy explained. "I asked a woman who can see and works with me at the factory, how much she spends for her electricity. She said they average about $27 each month. Because I am blind, I don't need light in my home, so I am taking the money I saved and giving it to the Lord so others can have the light instead.

Who is the light Kathy wanted others to see and know?

John 8:12

Then spake Jesus again unto them, saying, I am the light of the world: he that followeth me shall not walk in darkness, but shall have the light of life.

Growing older and having disabilities are part of aging. Thank God for granting me 96 years so far! Again, let me emphasize the necessity of surrounding yourself with godly people. I find comfort in Proverbs 20:29.

> The glory of young men is their strength; and the beauty of old men is the grey head.

God's Protection

While I was pastoring Bethany Baptist on New York Ave, a sixteen-year-old boy broke into the church one night looking for money or other things to steal and sell. He didn't find anything of value. So, in anger, he wadded up a paper bag, set it on fire, and put it in the corner of the building to set the building on fire. The whole building went up in flames. Much damage was done to the inside of the church but God's provision was evident.

For some reason, God protected a picture and frame. The fire folded the frame around the picture of Jesus praying in the garden. That may have been a sign or lesson for our church.

Anyway, it reminds me of the three Hebrew children, Daniel 3:27-30. They wouldn't bow, they wouldn't bend, and they wouldn't burn.

In the same way that God protected this picture, he protects your soul if you have him as your Lord and Savior.

> Psalm 121:1-2
>
> I will lift up mine eyes unto the hills, from whence cometh my help.
>
> My help cometh from the LORD, which made heaven and earth.

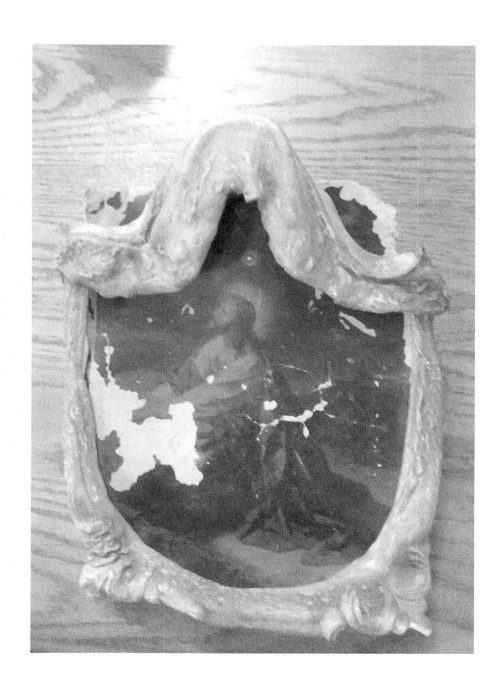

If I knew it would be the Last Time

If I knew it would be the last time that I'd see you fall asleep, I would tuck you in more tightly and pray the Lord your soul to keep.

If I knew it would be the last time that I'd see you walk out the door I would give you a hug and kiss and call you back for just one more.

If I knew it would be the last time that I'd hear your voice lifted up in praise, I would video tape each action and word so I could play them back day after day.

If I knew it would be the last time that I could spare an extra minute or two to stop and say, "I love You" instead of assuming you would know I do.

If I knew it would be the last time that I would be there to share your day, well I'm sure you have so many more, so I can let just this one slip away.

For surely there's always tomorrow to make up for an oversight and we always get a second chance to make everything right.

There will always be another day to say our "I love you" 's and certainly there's another chance to say our "Anything I can do" 's.

But just in case I might be wrong, and today is all I get, I should like to say how much I love you and I hope you never forget.

Tomorrow is not promised to anyone, young or old alike and today might be the last chance you get to hold your loved one tight.

So, if you are waiting for tomorrow, why not do it today? For if tomorrow never comes, you'll surely regret the day that you didn't take the extra time for a smile, a hug, or a kiss and you were too busy to grant someone, what turned out to be their last wish.

So hold your loved ones close today and whisper in their ear. Tell them how much you love them and that you'll always hold them dear.

Take time to say, "I'm sorry, please, forgive me, thank you, or its okay." And if tomorrow never comes, you'll have no regrets about today.

Have you lost someone dear to you and said to yourself, "I wish I had told them just how much I cared." Maybe you needed to ask someone for forgiveness. Maybe you had something you should have shared with them. Take the time now so you will have no regrets.

Thanks, Buddy Wimberly
(Pastor of Lanny Road Church, Florida)

Chapter 3: My family's Testimonies

God's truth endures to all generations....

Some of you who read my first book, *I Stake My Claim*, have asked about my children, "How have they turned out?" I am so very proud of them all. So, I asked each of them to write a short testimony for me to share in this new book. They all trusted Christ as their Savior when they were young. They have never been in jail or abused drugs or alcohol; and have been successful in raising wonderful children and grandchildren. I thank God for watching over them and blessing me with all of them.

I am proud to say, at least two of my grandsons are following me in answering God's call to preach the Gospel, Mark Shelby and Shannon Shelby.

Mark's Story was told in my first book. He and his family live in Mississippi now. You may know, we almost lost him a few years back. After taking a flu shot something went terribly wrong. He laid in the hospital for about six months with his arms and legs split open so that the muscles could get oxygen. Strange and horrible, but God took care of him and got him through it. Praise His Holy Name! God got his attention and called him to preach.

Michael Shannon Shelby is with Eternal Vision Ministry, singing and testifying wherever they are invited but located in Knoxville, TN. He not only is well known as lead singer, musician, and songwriter for the group but preaches revivals as well. His musical ability on piano, guitar, or whatever instrument, is truly a gift from God.

I keep lots of memories in my Bible like this one. When Shannon was a small boy, he sat in the pew listening to me preach. This is what he thought I looked like behind the pulpit. I might have lost a few pounds since then.

Family

I want my family to know that I thank God for them. I love my kids, grandkids and great grands, and great-great grands, and all that come later! God has surely blessed our family! I pray that each one will **Seek and Find God** and lead others to do the same.

From Left to Right: Stephen Victor, Gary Lynn, George Edward, Wiley Edward, Ruth Laurel, Deborah Ann, Michael Rand, Charles Eugene, Carden Dwayne

George Edward — The Firstborn of 7 kids

A little while back, Dad called and asked for something to be written for him. Since my middle name is procrastination, it took a few more calls. So here it goes.

- I can't preach.

- I can't sing.

- I can't play an instrument anymore.

- I can't even dance!

As you probably know by now, every one of my siblings were born with an exceptionally great talent. I was saved at the age of twelve at a service at Westside Baptist Church on Fifth Avenue in Knoxville Tennessee. With the exception of three years that I was in the U.S. Army, I followed Dad to the churches he pastored. One of them was Brushy Valley, where I met the young lady I married. Gladys Mae Wampler and I got married (by Dad) in 1964 and spent the next 52 years together until she passed away October 20, 2016. During that time, we were blessed with three children, Tony, Connie, and Dennis. We also were blessed with six grandchildren and eighteen great-grandchildren.

Gladys had some health problems which resulted in her passing away three times. The first time for 13 minutes. She was fifty years old the first time. She told me then not to worry—that she had seen heaven and its beauty, and that she was not afraid to die. When it happened the second time a few years later, she told me more again.

I can't tell you that everything has been perfect in my life. But I can tell you that God put me into one of the GREATEST families on earth. Maybe I was just put here to tell you that my God Is Good and these are my brothers and this is my sister, these are all Shelby Family. So, to sum up where I am after 77 years:

I still can't preach.

I still can't sing.

I still can't play an instrument.

I still can't dance.

BUT... I CAN STILL TALK WITH GOD AND I DO SEVERAL TIMES EVERY DAY.

Thanks, Dad, for everything you taught this family!

Love You,

George

Charles Eugene — 2nd Born Son

Me? I'm not a writer. Not much of a speaker, not much of an intellectual. But I guess I've never been too short on words, and never too shy about putting them out there either … I'm pretty sure that's what my old school friends and former co-workers would say about me. Anyone that grew up around me, or who got to know my young quick temper a little too intimately, or even those who just worked with me in my early days would say it for sure. I was one of those "loud 'n proud" guys who always had a viewpoint that was of course, correct, and I was not the least afraid to educate anyone about it. I guess it's possible that a lot of my close family would still tell you that's me, or at least, something along those lines. I was never one to be particularly soft in my approach to challenging an alternate opinion or discussion point. But growing up, as most people finally do, I think, I've changed quite a bit in the last half of my nearly 75-year-old life. Oh, I guess I still have too much to say from time to time, and maybe a little too sure of the absolute validity of my position, but maybe I've grown a little in the last few decades too. Maybe at least, I've learned to wait until the other person stops talking before I start. And maybe, I've learned to listen a little bit better too. These days, instead of projecting memorable lines from this play that's being written day by day, I'm so much more comfortable being in the audience, clapping, shouting hoo-rays … or just considering the point of the dialog of the person on center stage. This leads me to my point that when Dad first asked me to write a few words for his follow-up book, my first thought was that I don't have anything to add to his book … after all, it not about me. So, with that beginning of a few words, I'll add just a little bit to Dad's book …

Reading his words and his thoughts in his first collection of memories, reminded me of so much that I do know something about. I have since thought a lot about him and my mother, my brothers and sweet sister, my "Mamaw and Papaw", aunts, uncles and cousins … and about so many of the wonderful things that we shared as we learned to live life. Besides providing the usual things, like a roof over our heads, food and clothing, we were so blessed to have a Father and a Mother that cared for all our needs, whether natural or spiritual. Whether times were good and things were plentiful or times were not so good and the seven ill-favored and lean-fleshed kin were coming out of the river, we were a happy blessed family. And, our extended family were also hard working but just as poor in an economic sense, as were we. This is particularly true of those from "Mechanicsville" (a poor neighborhood in Knoxville, where the mill workers, iron workers, and sewing machine operators lived). But in spiritual riches, we were all so blessed that things of a material nature seemed not very important. My mother grew up in the Mechanicsville part of Knoxville. Her mother, "Mamaw" was one of the finest and most hardworking women you could possibly imagine. She was an inspiration. She was up before sunup cooking for everyone before they got out of bed, and before she headed off to work a full 8 to 10 hour day outside her home. She was an example Christian who everyone I knew looked up to and admired. She was loved and admired by all, because it was evident to all, that she not only talked the talk, but she walked the walk in every part of her Christian life. My Dad, My Mother, My Mamaw, so many Christian Aunts, Uncles, and others to influence my faith in Christ. Looking back now through the prism of all these years, I see even more clearly what a wonderful bunch of people to which God entrusted, not only my earthly care and natural needs, but entrusted those faithful people to focus His spiritual light on me as well. I could take hours to recount the wonderful people who have shaped my life, but since I cant's take hours here …

So let me just re-focus the light of these words on a few notables. I could mention the great Christian examples that I grew up around. I could mention the wonderful person in my life who God placed in my life as a wife, and who has been not only the love of my life, but a solid Christian inspiration and companion to me. She's been not only the best wife I could ever hope for, but she's been a wonderful Christian partner for me, as well. It would take much, much too long to tell just what she means to me, or to even scratch the surface of the topic of how much she has impacted my life. Faye and I raised five beautiful children with which God blessed us … and I do mean He blessed us with them … and doing so, much more than we could ever have imagined. We found very soon that God knew exactly how to bless us with the most perfect, lovely children for our own family. I'm so grateful for the important things in life that God has provided: children, family, a companion to share life with ... I could write a book on what my wife means to me and what a great influence she's been on my life ... but I guess I should get back to the few words I'm writing to Dad for his book update.

Of course, if you've read the preceding examples in his first book recalling some of the milestones of our lives and the blessings we enjoyed, you already know how important our parents were in guiding us through this life and illuminating the path that leads to Christ. We kids had first hand examples that educated us as to in whom we should put our eternal trust. We were able to see up close how God could strengthen one's faith through times of adversity and it was an invaluable life's lesson ... It was an invaluable lesson about coming to Christianity as well. Through our parents, we could see how God would not only supply our needs (as He does the sparrow), but would bless us richly in the important things, such as family and our relationship with Him. As a young boy I knew I wanted to follow Christ, and I had parents that helped clear the path leading to a relationship with Him. Of course, as with most of us prodigals, it was way too easy to slip off the path and into the weeds, and I am certainly no exception. But because of all my parents had poured into me since I was old enough to remember, it was always clear to me what path God wanted me on, and that He would be there for me. My Mother and Dad built the foundation that allowed me to reach and realize a personal relationship with Christ. From that foundation many others in my life have added support, allowing a stronger more fulfilling walk with Him. Many have played a role of Christian support in my life ... some a little, some quite a lot. I'm grateful for them all. I'm sure God will place a few stars in their crown. And as I reflect on my few words for Dad's book update .... maybe all of this was more about me than I thought!

Thank you, God, for the wonderful Christian examples you've placed in my life.

Love you Dad,

Charles

Gary Lynn — 3rd Born Son

My Life in Gospel Music and the Service of Our LORD.

By Gary L. Shelby, Sr.

Every gospel singer has someone that they say has inspired them to sing and praise the LORD. Well, I am no exception. The only difference is that I have more than one who has inspired me to sing.

Let me start from the beginning. I had always sung in church, the choir, solos and with other singers in the church, including my family. But, when my brother, Mike began singing with his wife, Susan, and my brother Dwayne, I felt a longing that would continue until this day. Mike has a way about him that you know that he is gifted of God and that he is singing for Him. Every time that I got the opportunity to go with them to a singing, and help them, whether it be to setup equipment or sing a song or two, I took advantage. So, I guess that I would say that Mike is one of those that have inspired me to sing.

Then there is my Dad and Mom. Having been taken to church from the time I was born, I was among the church singers a lot. Dad always taught us kids that we are to sing praises; as he puts it, "Make a joyful noise to the LORD." Through his leadership, singing, preaching, he inspired me to follow that desire and begin singing. Mother always had a word of encouragement for me and she would say, I am very proud of what you kids are doing."

And lastly, the most important, Our LORD and Savior, Jesus Christ. With the desire that He put in my heart and the voice He gave to me, I finally decided that I needed to get busy about the work that He had for me.

Starting in the late seventies, one of the first groups that I sang with was a local group called "The Crossmen". I wasn't with them very long; it just didn't seem to satisfy the longing in my heart. Then, I began singing with a group called "The Anchormen". With this group I traveled through the southern and middle part of the country. While with them, we saw many, many souls saved and converted from a life of sin, by the Grace of God. Also, I got a chance to have my oldest son, Lynn, travel with me as a member of the band playing the keyboard. That was an added blessing. This lasted for about eleven and a half years, before I started to feel that God was through with me there. So, I left in search of the next.

After a short time of searching, I found "Eternal Vision Ministries" in 1991. It started out as a need for me to play bass guitar for a weekend while Gail (Mike's wife and the bass player) was supposed to be recuperating from surgery. But, she stated that the bus was not leaving Knoxville without her. When we got to Kentucky, the bass singer, Darrell Lucas, asked Mike what they were going to do with me since Gail was determined to play bass. Mike replied, "I guess we will have to let him sing." That was the start of seeing many a sinner saved by Grace and the receipt of multiple years of blessings.

I remember in 2001, I was having some health problems and wound up having a stent placed in a main artery of my heart. When I was told that I needed the surgery, I never had a second thought about the outcome. I knew that God had everything in His hands. Though at that time it was serious, I told my family that I was not afraid to die because I knew where I was headed if I did. God had everything covered. When my doctor came to release me from the hospital, he told Mike that I was crazy, and of course, Mike said that he already knew that. But my doctor said, "No, I mean he *IS* really crazy. He thinks that he is going to Florida this weekend to sing."

Mike's reply, "Well, he probably will. He's just that crazy." I went that weekend, sang and God blessed. I never slowed down until in 2005, then the company where I worked told me that I would have to sing or work, not both. Since I had bills to pay and gospel music didn't pay the bills, I had to retire from Eternal Vision Ministries. Don't get me wrong, God has never let me go hungry or without but I felt that is was time.

After a few years, and a change of employers, I had an opportunity to sing with "The Supernals" from Maryville, TN. I only sang with them for maybe a year but we had many blessed meetings, and then I felt that God was through with me there. I have worked with choirs at church, the youth and sang solos and that longing for the harmony of voices is still calling. There is nothing like that Southern Gospel Music sound.

So that is just a little of my life in gospel music. But it is not the end. God has a work for each of us and I am searching for my next one. As my Dad once said, "There is no retiring from the work God has for us, only rest."

Pray for all those that are in the service of our LORD and Savior, Jesus Christ.

Gary

Note from Wiley: I see that Gary forgot to tell one important thing he did when he was about one year old. I was working at Oak Ridge and Imogene (Mother), took him to visit her aunt Pearl Housewright. They were hanging curtains and had a hammer and some nails laying on the floor nearby. Of course, a child will grab whatever he finds to play with. Gary very quickly stuffed one nail in his mouth before anyone could get it away. He actually swallowed a #4 Penny Nail! Imogene took him to Saint Mary's Hospital, where doctors took x-rays and watched the nail going through Gary's system. They fed him macaroni and cheese with corn bread, hoping to turn the nail head-side-down. That way it might safely pass through Gary's system and they would not have to operate ... Praise God, it worked! Thank You Jesus!!!

Stephen Victor – 4th Born Son

<u>Note from Wiley:</u> Steve has written several poems and important works. He is known in our family for his telling of tall tales and retelling the Christmas story. His godly character can be seen throughout his work. Enjoy!

One day, while Steve and I were deer hunting together, we found this little country church in Catoosa Hunting Area. That's in Cumberland Mountain. Yes, I know country churches back then were small because few people lived in the mountains. They had to walk or ride horses to get there. The LORD was with them because He said in Matthew 18:20

"For where two or three are gathered together in my name, there am I in the midst of them."

Reflections of an old Country Church

By Steve Shelby

My weathered logs stand idle, now
No songs within are sung
My benches are no longer used
My rusty bell unrung.

My shutters are all broken now,
The door was left ajar,
My rafters moan in the winter wind.
My shingles blown afar.

My littered floor with leaves and dirt,
Which once was laid with care,
Now home for tiny creatures wild
That seek strong shelter there.

The woods are creeping closer now
With passing of the years.
The briars in my graveyard
Would bring a man to tears.

Weeds and brush have overgrown
The pathway to my door.
Rotted steps up to my porch
Will creak and groan no more.

The painted name above my entrance
Long ago did fade.
But the Rock of My Foundation
Is as strong as when first laid.

Sundays brought the families in
From all the farms around.
In summer there'd be all day meetings
And dinner on the ground.

With boys catching crawdads
In the creek that flows outback.
And sneaking down the ladies' path
For a look through outhouse cracks.

In Spring, love notes across the pews
Were passed by giggly girls.
To red faced boys who after church,
Would tug their golden curls.

Autumn bounty shared with neighbors,
Pickles changed for beets,
Quiltin' bees and shuckings,
A place for friends to meet.

Winter brought the old coal stove,
By the deacon's bench and water gourd.
When the temperature dropped,
They all moved up a little closer to the Lord.

Their "Sunday-go-to-meetin" shoes
Would shine with fresh rubbed lard.
They'd visit after church
And hunker down out in the yard.

Old Aunt Pearl, when she came in,
Would take a dip of snuff.
And never spit throughout the service
Holding in the stuff.

Til after meetin', she'd walk out,
Two fingers to her lips,
And shoot a stream full twenty feet
While down her chin it dripped.

When they sang, my rafters rang,
"Nearer My God to thee" and "Victory in Jesus"
The voices shook my window panes
And the Holy Ghost would seize us.

Old Ms. Campbell would lift her hands,
Throw back her head and scream.
Brother Moore shouted "Hallelujah!"
And "Praise the King."

Then behind "The Book" a husky man
With jet black hair would stand,
Take off his coat, loose his tie
And spread apart his hands.

He'd preach "The Loaves and Fishes"
Or perhaps "The Prodigal Son".
Genesis to Revelation
Would be hit before he was done.

Hell-fire and brimstone
Would cause their hair to raise.
A sinner-man within my walls
Could feel the licking blaze.

When they felt they all were doomed,
He'd tell of the city above.
A smile would spread across his face.
As he told of Jesus' love.

With arms spread wide this earthly guide,
Would give it all his best.
"Oh, ye that are heavy laden," he cried,
"Come unto me and rest."

Down the aisle a young man would run,
Pounding heart would crave,
Fall on his knees, bow down his head,
Begging to be saved.

The Amen corner would then burst forth,
As if they had their cue.
Brother Knight, when feeling right,
Would dance across the pew.

"Amazing Grace" poured out in song
From all the heavenly bound,
As vigorous handshakes all confirmed
Another lost sheep was found.

My weathered logs stand idle now,
No songs within are sung.
My benches are no longer used
My rusty bell unrung.

The painted name above my entrance
Long ago did fade.
But the Rock of My foundation
Is as strong as when first laid.

###

Deborah Ann Shelby Godfrey — 5th born and only daughter!

As I sit to write a short testimony for my Daddy's new book, I just learned that his first book is on display in a bookstore near me! I am so proud of my Daddy! Someday, he will be leaving such a legacy for our family and friends; such a witness for God for generations to follow. I hope and pray that I will be like him when I am 96 years old, living by faith, still actively pursuing God's plan for my life. I strongly believe that it is our responsibility to pass on our faith to upcoming generations, as he has done. Be an example, live by faith—and tell others what God has done for me personally. The scriptures and the Holy Spirit will do the rest. Hebrews 11-12 gives us many examples of our predecessors who lived "**BY FAITH**".

My parents provided a strong Christian foundation in my upbringing; following Proverbs 22:6, "Train up a child in the way he should go, and when he is old he will not depart from it". We were taught to live always serving, witnessing, and trusting God as our main purpose in life. Singing and playing the piano was my gift. My brothers were all in the school band, but I remember Daddy saying, "Debbie's piano lessons are so she can play in church!" And, from a very young age I was doing that every chance I got. I even played and sang on Daddy's Saturday afternoon WKXV radio broadcast for many, many years.

I firmly believe that my early years formed my solid Christian foundation. We were always heavily involved in church plays, Sunday School, Bible studies, "Saturday Night Singings", funerals, weddings, Bible School, etc. This involvement carried over into my school life. In High School, I loved Bible class and researched and wrote an impressive report on "Women in the Church". This was a little progressive at that time, but I knew God could use me as he did many wonderful women in the Bible. While attending University of Tennessee for business, all my extra credits were in Religious Studies. After marriage and college, I continued studying the Holy Scriptures in various formats, including years in Bible Study Fellowship. My faith in God continues to sustain me through good and bad times — because you have to know what is in the Bible to know your Savior! How can you believe if you do not do the research?

> Matthew 7:8
>
> For every one that asketh receiveth; and he that seeketh findeth; and to him that knocketh it shall be opened.

Yes, I too am like my father, living By Faith! Trying to do the same for my children and grandkids. I am not perfect, but I hunger and thirst for righteousness. I may have inherited my love for Christ; but I believe that God is faithful. His promises are fulfilled through His Son, Jesus Christ our Redeemer. I have confidence that God has _and_ will provide the perfect plan. That's called Trust. And as I face life's challenges, my strength comes from knowing that I am a child of God. *"Let all that I am praise the LORD!"*

Debbie

Psalm 100

Make a joyful shout to the LORD, all you lands! [2]Serve the LORD with gladness: come before His presence with singing. [3]Know that the LORD, He is God; It is He who has made us, and not we ourselves; We are His people and the sheep of His pasture. [4]Enter into His gates with thanksgiving, And into His courts with praise. Be thankful to Him, and bless His name.

[5]For the LORD is good; His mercy is everlasting, and His truth endures to all 3generations.

Michael Rand – 6th born (5th son)

My testimony is best summarized in the words of David,

> Psalm 16:6
>
> The lines are fallen unto me in pleasant places;
> yea, I have a goodly heritage.

I am convinced that so many of the Lord's blessings upon my life can be attributed to the faithfulness of my parents. They laid the foundation and instilled within me The Holy Word of God that has sustained and sheltered me through the fiercest of storms.

From being diagnosed with an inoperable brain tumor in the year 2000, and given as little as three years to live, to a quintuple open heart bypass surgery, to the early passing of My wife in 2016. Time and time again God faithfully carried me through. Just like the verse I first heard from my Daddy years ago,

> Psalm 55:22
>
> Cast your burden on the Lord, and he will sustain you; he will never permit the righteous to be moved.

Our God is faithful!

I have been blessed with Godly parents and a good heritage! For that, I give God glory! He has shown me kindness that I sure don't deserve. I am truly grateful for parents that allowed God to work in them, and in my life!

My gratitude must lead to action. I pray that I can pass the baton to the next generation. That a goodly heritage will be handed down to my children. That someday my children will speak about me the way I speak about my parents. I pray the same for whoever reads this book. And if you're unable to see the Godly line in your history, start one! Let the future generations look back at you and say, "The lines are fallen unto me in pleasant places; yea, I have a goodly heritage."

Daddy, thanks for giving me more than love. Thank you for showing me Jesus.

I praise God for you and for "a goodly heritage."

Your son,

Mike

Carden Dwayne — The Youngest of 7 kids

I love to collect instruments, any kind I can get my hands on. I like to try to learn to play them. I'm not always the best at it, but I love music. My love of music started when I was about six years old. My family has always been involved in music. My Dad had a gospel radio program on Saturdays from 3 to 3:30 PM on WKXV am 900. I grew up going every Saturday. My sister Debbie would be playing the piano. My brother Mike and I would be in the audience, listening. At times my family would sing on the program and that was an exciting time for me.

My desire for music caused me to ask Mike, who had learned to play the piano, if he would teach me. So, I learned to play the piano and guitar when I was six.

As Debbie got older and married Bill, Mike filled the vacant spot as the piano player at church and on the radio program. Then, Mike got older and got a job working at White Stores on Saturdays. So, I moved into his place to play piano for my Dad.

From time to time, Dad, Mother, and I (and Mike — if he was around) would sing on the radio and at church. Often, we would go to gospel singings on Fridays and Saturdays. People would invite Dad to preach at revivals where we would also sing. So basically, everything in my world was surrounded by music.

Later, Mike and Cousin Alan had a gospel group called "the Gospel Lights". They invited me to play the piano for them. Mike played guitar and Alan played the bass. Their wives also sang with them. We had pretty decent harmony. I did that for several years and really enjoyed it. We recorded a couple of albums, in which included some of the songs I wrote. The title song, "Jesus Is the One Who Took the Cross of Calvary" was one of the very first songs I wrote — and it sounded really good on the album. I loved being able to record.

As years went by, things happened and "Gospel Light" dispersed. I was left with no group. A lot of people in Knoxville had heard me sing and I was given several opportunities to fill in for different groups.

One of the most memorable was with the Anchormen out of Maryville which my brother, Gary, had sung with in the past. His son, Lynn, had played piano for them. I sang tenor for the group. We traveled to Florida, South Carolina, Georgia, North Carolina, Kentucky, and parts of Tennessee. I think we even went to Alabama. It was a lot of traveling and I was not used to it. I was married and things were really busy. I decided I didn't want to travel out of town anymore.

I was also given an opportunity to sing with a newly formed group in Knoxville by the name of "Christian Heart". The group had been known as a Southern Gospel group by another name. The guitar player, Denny Evans, went to the church where Daddy pastored, at Bon View Baptist. I met one of my best friends, Kevin Connatser, who was in the group. And Dan Hensley was the bass player. "Christian Heart" gradually changed from strictly Southern Gospel to a mixture of Southern Gospel and Christian Country or Country Gospel.

As time progressed, we recorded albums and did some traveling. It wasn't quite as much traveling as with the Anchormen, but I was beginning to open up to more traveling. Gradually the group changed and as always people come and go. The final group wound up with a very Christian Country sound, basically country music with a Christian meaning. We were able to witness to more people with this genre. I really enjoyed doing that style of music. You pretty much could put it up against anything on the country station and it would crossover a lot of it. We got God's message out, too.

With all the songs, we saw a lot of people saved and a lot of people rededicating their lives to Jesus. Also, we had a lot of people who followed the group, would buy albums, and wear T-shirts with our name on them. We had some good "Roadies". We had buses, then we had cars, and trailers. We would basically just go with the times, whatever was most convenient at that time, whether we were traveling a lot or a little, but we really had a good time.

That group finally ended with Kevin Connatser on the drums, and the late Ted Lowe, Jr. on the guitar—very talented guy. (He was also radio station manager at WKXV, where Dad used to have his radio program.) There was also Todd Hazelwood and Charlie Caylor. We were able to do quite a bit with that group. We actually got to record a professional recording at what used to be Conway Twitty's recording studio. What an experience we had! All professional instrument players. Some cuts from that album were actually played on some national radio stations. We even had a manager.

One of the highlights with that band was when I got to sing at Cowboy Church in Nashville Tennessee and where I got to meet Johnny Cash's sister. Sometime around the late 90's, the group died out. Everyone went their way.

Since then, I have sung some in churches, off and on, but I haven't been back with a group. However, God blessed me with a wonderful wife, Chasity, who can sing fabulously. I love singing with her from time to time as we get to sing in church.

Dwayne

I'll Take the Road to Heaven

By Dwayne Shelby

On this road that we're on,
decisions must be made...
Some don't seem that much
while others seem too great.
The most important thing in life
that we must decide,
is the road that we'll take
and where we will arrive.

Well as for me, I'll take the road to Heaven,
Yes, I'll walk that straight and narrow way.
And you can make the step into the right direction
when you take the glory road.
Just follow in the footsteps of the LORD.

Only you can choose which road you take.
Is it the wide and winding road
with curves that blind your way?
Or will you take the straight road
that narrow and bright,
Where Heaven is your destiny,
and the Lamb is your light?

<u>Note from Wiley:</u> At fifteen years old, my son wrote this as
his first song.

Testimonial from My Lovely Bride

Ruth's story

Over seven years ago, my daughter Sandra lived and worked in Florida. There she met Rev. Wiley Shelby and Eternal Vision singers visiting at her church. The EV group announced they were to perform at Christmas in the Smokies in Pigeon Forge, Tennessee. So, Sandra called me to come meet Wiley and EV at the event. (At the time, I was living in North Carolina with my son Michael and his wife, Cyndi.) I went to meet them in Tennessee.

Sandra introduced me to Wiley while he was sitting at the EV information table selling their music, etc. He asked me to help at the table and I agreed! We got acquainted and two months later we got married. We have been married happily for 7 years currently and thank God for each day. In Wiley's first book, *I Stake My Claim*, he tells about our meeting and courtship. To find out more about this and early events in his life, you need to read that book.

I was raised on Long Island, New York. My first husband (Arthur Johansen) and I were married 63 years before he passed away. We had five children together, Michael, Patrick, Laurie, Sandra, and Mark. Laurie was born with Down Syndrome. It was through Laurie at this difficult time that I came to take Jesus as my personal savior.

She died at six months old.

We got involved with foster care babies and eventually adopted a brother and sister: Dennis and Cassie. So that made seven children in our family (counting Laurie in Heaven), same as in Wiley's family! And according to their testimony, all my children claim Jesus as their Savior, too.

Unlike Wiley's kids who stayed in Tennessee (except for George in Alabama), my kids scattered across the United States... mostly for their jobs. They continue to be a blessing to me and I send my love to each of them!

- Michael & Cyndi (wife) in Indiana

- Patrick & Carla (wife) in Washington State

- Sandra & Tom (husband) in Tennessee

- Mark in Michigan

- Dennis & Jamie (wife) in Virginia

- Cassie in Alabama

Left to right: Debby Halgren (niece), Carol Fasano (niece),
Cyndi Johansen (daughter-in-law), Michael Johansen (son),
Arianna Armentrout (granddaughter), Mark Johansen (son),
Wiley (husband), Ruth (self), Cassie Stetson (daughter),
Brittany Stetson (granddaughter), Sandra Turner (daughter),
Tom Turner (son-in-law)

Cabin Creek

There is a place where a creek swells up
   and runs wildly through the woods.
It steals the leaves that cross its path
   and ignores where the old oak stood.
The majestic pines race toward the sky
   just to see who'll get there first.
They greet the clouds that split apart
   to let the sunshine burst.
The morning dew drips off a leaf
   to awaken a wildflower.
The sunny breeze carry the butterflies
   to the clearing where they gather.
Amidst the brush, behind the fog
   the spiders weave their nests.
And when they're done, they've little cradles
   that rock them while they rest.
So God has placed the setting
   where the ray of sunshine streaks.
We've made our home beneath Him
   and we call it Cabin Creek.

-Cassandra Stetson-

Serving Our Country

I might say a few words about my family serving our country in time of war and peace.

James E. (Jim) Shelby, WW1, son of Ebb Shelby of Sharps Chapel

My dad served in the Army in World War 1. I will not go into any of the stories of combat he was in. James E. Jim Shelby, WW 1, son of Ebb Shelby of Sharps Chapel, Tennessee.

My brother Leroy Shelby served in the Navy in World War 2. He and his gun crew went down on the USS Luce due to Japanese bombing the ship.

I served in the Army during World War 2, in training camps in the US.

My son George served in the Army overseas from September 1962 to September 1965.

My son Steve served overseas in the Marines.

Thank God for all who serve and protect our country.

Eternal Vision

Let me introduce you to Eternal Vision Ministry. They have been an important part of our journey.

In November 1989, a determined group of people joined hands with each other and God to form Eternal Vision Ministry. My son, Mike Shelby, got the group together to seek the leadership of the LORD. The purpose in their hearts was to put His Will into motion and to see lost people come to Christ. All members being raised from childhood in gospel music, felt the presence of God forming something more than just another singing group—but, they had no idea what God had in store for them.

They believed that as God has called ministers to pastor churches, He has called them into a ministry field of spreading His Word in testimony and song. They have one objective, that is to see lost souls accept Christ as their personal Savior. God has worked in their ministry in many places, including churches, parking lots, theaters, concert hall, auditoriums, and anywhere else that He has opened the door for them. They have seen many, many souls come to Jesus.

The group would appreciate your attendance anywhere that they are going to perform. They covet your prayers and love offerings. Without this, they could not continue this work that God has given them to do. They operate solely on donations. They do not set a fee for them to attend your church. They feel each church knows the expenses and sets a goal. God will supply the need for His job to be accomplished.

My grandson, Shannon Shelby is the lead singer, plays the piano with his hands, and sometimes his foot on the keyboard. Any instrument you hand him he can play. (Mike also plays any instrument and is self-taught, or God-taught.). Last, but not least, God called Shannon to preach about four or five years ago.

Over the years, singers joined them but came and went, some through sickness, death, etc. Now the group singers are Mike as alto, Shannon as lead, Warren Beeler as tenor, and Danny Overholt as bass. I am so proud of them all and not only them but their families. They let them travel just about every weekend and support them with their prayers.

Chapter 4: Final Thoughts

I Have a Note for You!

By Rev Wiley Shelby

I have been a Christian a long time and I am kept by a precious friend of mine, Jesus.

But when I find myself faltering along the way, I just look up to Jesus and ask Him to carry me in His strong arms. He knows just what I need!

It doesn't matter if you are old or young, struggles reach everyone in this life. Does it seem like the devil is working overtime on you? Constantly putting troubles in your way, causing more problems for you ... I have good news to bring! Just for you!

Our Heavenly Father is working overtime too.

When it seems that everything in your life has gone wrong.

The devil is on your back, all day long,

and you just can't go on ...

That's when the LORD works overtime once again – to make you strong!

HE CARES

Looking around at all the sadness in the world, it sometime seems that the evil outweighs the good. But there is hope when God's love is unfurled. For He Cares and will be there for you like he said. He will never leave you nor forsake you. (Hebrews 13:5, Genesis 28:15)

Sometimes it seems like all hope is gone. We think we can't win the battles of this life that we try to face all alone. But there is one God who holds the answer to all things. He watches over us with His mercy and grace. He cares when no one else does, for He love us.

Romans 5:8 says:

> But God commendeth his love toward us, in that, while we were yet sinners, Christ died for us.

We need to learn to lean on Jesus. He is a wall of strength for all who believe. He is there to lean on for any need. But if your faith falters and you are feeling like you might fall, remember it is you who moved and not our strong LORD. Lean on Jesus and you can't go wrong.

> Hebrews 4:16
>
> Let us therefore come boldly unto the throne of grace, that we may obtain mercy, and find grace to help in time of need.

How To Be 100% Sure You are Going to Heaven

We live in troubled times. This world offers no peace. Money offers no peace. Not even church or family offers true peace. True peace and joy are only found in the LORD Jesus Christ.

If you realize that something is missing in your life, then I ask you to invite Jesus to be the LORD of your life. Invite Him into your heart. He can give you Eternal Life. He can give you peace and joy. Jesus loves you so much that He gave His life for you on the cross. If you ask Him, He will come into your life. If you reject Him, then you have rejected the only hope available!

> 1 John 5:13
>
> These things have I written unto you that believe on the name of the Son of God; that ye may know that ye have eternal life, and that ye may believe on the name of the Son of God.

First, know that sin separates us from God!

Realize the consequence of *your* sin. Acknowledge we are all sinners.

> Romans 3:23
>
> For all have sinned, and come short of the Glory of God.

The Holy Scriptures goes on to say that sin keeps us from having a personal relationship with God.

Isaiah 59:2

But your iniquities have separated between you
and your God, and your sins have hid His face
from you, that he will not hear.

Sadly, our sin separates us from God not only in this
life but for all eternity! Death and Hell awaits...

Romans 6:23

For the wages of sin is death; but the gift of God
is eternal life through Jesus Christ our LORD.

Jesus clearly stated that the <u>only</u> way to God is
through his death and resurrection,

John 14:6

"I am the Way, the Truth, and The Life, No
man cometh unto the Father, but by me."

Romans 5:8

But God commendeth His love toward us, in
that while we were yet sinners, Christ died for
us.

Second, Jesus overcame sin and death as our Redeemer!

Acknowledge the sacrifice of Jesus Christ made for
us. He paid our sin debt in full on the cross. God is
not willing for anyone to experience eternity
without Him. Jesus died for us!

2 Peter 3:9

> The LORD is ... not willing that any should perish, but that all should come to repentance.

Third, accept God's gift of eternal life by faith in Jesus's blood sacrifice.

Simply <u>ask</u> God to save you from your sin. Repent and believe in Christ's sacrifice for us.

> John 3:16
>
> For God so love the world that He gave His only begotten son, that whosoever believeth in Him should not perish but have everlasting life.
>
> Romans 10:9
>
> That if thou shalt confess with thy mouth the Lord Jesus, and shalt believe in thine heart that God hath raised Him from the dead, thou shalt be saved.

Paul told the early churches in one of his letters that "we are in the last days". And if he preached that *then*— what are we in now? We surely today live in turbulent times, but Jesus calls, "Come unto me", just as you are. If you acknowledge that something is missing in your life, pray now. Ask Jesus Christ to come into your life. Ask Him to save you. He can give you peace, joy, and eternal life. He loved you so much that He died for you and me. He paid a debt you nor I could ever pay! He is the only peace on this earth and the only peace after the death of this body.

Jesus explained to Nicodemus, "Except a man be born of water and of the Spirit, he cannot enter into the kingdom of God. That which is born of the flesh is flesh; and that which is born of the Spirit is spirit."

John 3:1-7

There was a man of the Pharisees, named Nicodemus, a ruler of the Jews:

The same came to Jesus by night, and said unto him, Rabbi, we know that thou art a teacher come from God: for no man can do these miracles that thou doest, except God be with him.

Jesus answered and said unto him, Verily, verily, I say unto thee, Except a man be born again, he cannot see the kingdom of God.

Nicodemus saith unto him, How can a man be born when he is old? can he enter the second time into his mother's womb, and be born?

Jesus answered, Verily, verily, I say unto thee, Except a man be born of water and of the Spirit, he cannot enter into the kingdom of God.

That which is born of the flesh is flesh; and that which is born of the Spirit is spirit.

Marvel not that I said unto thee, Ye must be born again.

And as believers and His followers, Jesus left us specific instructions and reassurance!

Matthew 28:19-20

Go ye therefore, and teach all nations, baptizing them in the name of the Father, and of the Son, and of the Holy Ghost; Teaching them to observe all things whatsoever I have commanded you: and, lo, I am with you always, even unto the end of the world. Amen.

Heaven can be your home! Choose wisely!

...And may God bless you out of His abundant riches,

And if I may say it,

"Wow, Ain't God Good!!!"

Rev. Wiley E. Shelby

Made in the USA
Monee, IL
09 May 2023